The Beast

Brandon Robshaw

Published in association with
The Basic Skills Agency

Hodder Murray
A MEMBER OF THE HODDER HEADLINE GROUP

Orders: please contact Bookpoint Ltd, 130 Milton Park, Abingdon, Oxon OX14 4SB.
Telephone: (44) 01235 827720. Fax: (44) 01235 400454. Lines are open 9.00–6.00,
Monday to Saturday, with a 24-hour message answering service. Visit our website at
www.hoddereducation.co.uk

© Brandon Robshaw 2005
First published in 2005 by
Hodder Murray, a member of the Hodder Headline Group
338 Euston Road
London NW1 3BH

Impression number 10 9 8 7 6 5 4 3 2 1
Year   2010 2009 2008 2007 2006 2005

Illustrations: Pulsar Studio/Beehive Illustration.
Cover illustration: Janos Jantner/Beehive Illustraion.
Typeset by Transet Limited, Coventry, England.
Printed in Great Britain by Athenaeum Press Ltd, Gateshead, Tyne & Wear.

A catalogue record for this title is available from the British Library

ISBN-10 340 90058 X
ISBN-13 9 780340 900581

Contents

1

The Beast Strikes Again

'Do you want to make some money?'
asked Dave.

His friend Nick looked at him.
'What do you mean, make some money?'

'I mean, make some money,' said Dave.
'Lots of it.'

They were in the store-room
of the supermarket where they worked.
They stacked the shelves.
It wasn't very well paid.
But at least it was a job.

Right now it was their tea-break.
They were sitting on boxes drinking tea.

'How are we going to make lots of money?'
asked Nick.

Dave held out the paper he had been reading.
'Look,' he said.

Nick wasn't much of a one for reading.
But he could make out the headline.
'BEAST OF THE MOORS STRIKES AGAIN'
Next to it was a picture of a dead horse
lying in a field.

'What's that about, then?' asked Nick.
'Someone's killed a horse?'

'Not someone,' said Dave.
'It's the Beast of the Moors.
Down in the West Country.
There's this great big animal on the moors.
Some sort of big cat.
Like a puma or something.
It keeps killing ponies.'

'Rubbish!' said Nick.
'Pumas don't live in this country.
How did it get there?'

'No one really knows.
Maybe someone bought it as a pet.
Then, when it got too big to look after,
they turned it loose on the moor.
Maybe.'

Nick looked at the piece in the paper again.
'Why isn't there a picture of it?'

'That's the whole point!' said Dave.
'There aren't any pictures of it!
No one's ever taken one.
If we went down there and got a photo of it,
we'd be rich!
Every newspaper in the country
would want it.
We'd make thousands.'

Nick scratched his head. He was thinking.
'Suppose we found this Beast,' he said slowly.
'And then it ate us.'

'Don't be stupid!' said Dave.
'It won't eat us!'

Just then Mr Dale, their boss, came in.
He clapped his hands.
'Come on lads, back to work!
Those shelves won't stack themselves!'

Nick stood up. He finished his tea.
Then he looked at Dave.
'OK,' he said. 'I'm in.'

2

A Trip to the Moors

The train pulled into the station.
It was a little country station.
The platform was empty.

Dave and Nick got out.
It was raining. The sky was dark grey.

They both had rucksacks.
Dave was also carrying a tent.
They were going to camp on the moors.

'It's a bit wet for camping,' said Nick,
looking up at the dark grey sky.

'Don't you worry,' said Dave.
'It's worth getting a bit wet
to make tens of thousands of pounds.'

It was a few days after their talk at work.
They had taken a week's holiday
from the supermarket.
For their summer break, they said.

They walked into the village.
It was right on the edge of the moor.
There was a pub, a church
and a post office and general store.
Not much else.

'Let's go to the post office,' said Dave.
'We can buy some food and stuff for later.
We can ask if anyone knows about the Beast.'

'OK,' said Nick.
'Anything to get out of the rain.'

They walked into the post office
and general store.
There was a queue of people
waiting at the counter.
They all turned and stared at Dave and Nick.

3
Sound Advice

'Hi,' said Dave.
For a long time, nobody said anything.
They all just stared at Dave and Nick.
Someone coughed.
At last, one old woman
nodded her head slightly.
'Morning.'

'Well, let's get some stuff,' said Dave.
He didn't like being stared at.
He tried to hide it by speaking loudly.
'We'll need some bread and milk and cheese.'

'And chocolate,' said Nick.

They joined the queue.
'We're here on holiday,' said Dave
to the man next to him.

'Really,' said the man.
He had a beard and wore an old cap.

'We're going to camp on the moors,'
said Dave.

There was another long silence.
Dave could feel every eye in the room
upon him.

'I wouldn't do that if I were you,'
said the man in the cap at last.

'Why not?' said Dave.
'Because of the Beast?'

Everyone in the room breathed in sharply.
'We don't talk about that here,'
said the woman behind the counter.

'Is it true?' asked Nick. 'Is there a Beast?'

'If you camp out on the moor,
you'll find out,' said the man in the cap.
'But I wouldn't if I were you.'

'Has anyone here seen it?' asked Dave.

'You just leave the Beast alone,
and it'll leave you alone,'
said the woman behind the counter.

Nobody would say anything more
about the Beast.
Dave paid for the food.
He and Nick walked out of the shop in silence.

'They were just trying to scare us,' said Dave.

'I'd say they succeeded,' said Nick.

4
A Dark Shape

Dave and Nick walked to the edge
of the village.
There was the moor – big and wide and empty.
A grey mist hung over it.

'Look, there's a path,' said Dave.
'Let's follow it.'

'I don't like this,' said Nick.
'It's creepy.'

'Don't worry about that,' said Dave.
'Think of those hundreds of thousands
of pounds we're going to get.'

They walked over the moor.
Soon, the village was out of sight.
The mist got thicker.
Somewhere, a bird gave a sad, lonely call.

Dave had his camera at the ready.
Nick didn't have a camera,
but he had a mobile that took pictures.

'I hope we see it in this mist,' said Dave.
'I'm not sure I want to see it,' said Nick.

They walked on.
Dave grabbed Nick's arm.
'What's that?'

There was a dark shape ahead.
Nick's heart started beating hard.

They went nearer.
The dark shape didn't move.
It was lying on the ground.
It was a dead pony.
Or what was left of it.

5
A Noise in the Night

'I don't like this,' said Nick.
'Let's get out of here.
Let's go back to the station.'

'Are you mad?' said Dave.
'This shows we're on the right track.
It must be near here.'

He looked around.
There was no sign of the Beast.
But he couldn't see far in the mist.

'Let's put the tent up here,' said Dave.
'It may come back
to eat the rest of the pony.
And then we'll get a picture!'

'And then we'll get eaten,' said Nick.

'No, we won't,' said Dave.
'It will be scared away by the camera flash.'

They put the tent up.
They ate some bread and cheese.
They had chocolate for afters.

By this time it was dark.
They were tired from the long walk
over the moor.
They got into the tent.
They fell asleep straight away.

Around midnight, they both woke up.
Nick grabbed Dave's arm.
'What's that noise?'

It was the noise of a beast roaring,
not far away.

6

Lost on the Moor

Dave sat up. He grabbed his camera.
'Let's go!'

'What?' said Nick. 'Are you mad?
Go out there now? It will eat you up!'

'It'll be OK,' said Dave.
'Come on, this is our big chance!'

'I'm not going out there!'

'Suit yourself,' said Dave.
'Stay there if you're scared.
I'll go on my own!'

He crawled out of the tent.
It was cold outside. It was still misty.
He couldn't see the stars.
The moon was a faint glow.

He heard the roar again.
He walked towards it, camera at the ready

After a while, he heard the roar again.
Now it was further away.
Dave turned towards it.

He walked on.
He heard the roar one more time,
very faint and far away.

He walked on for a bit
but he didn't hear the roar again.
He must have heard wrong.
It was hard to tell where sounds
were coming from in the mist.

He had better go back to the tent.
He turned and set off the way he had come.
But was it the way he had come?
He walked and walked
but he could not see the tent.
He was lost.

The ground started to get soft.
His feet were sinking in.
He tried to go back.
At the next step he sank up to his knees.

He was in a bog.
He had heard tales of people
falling into these bogs.
They slowly sank and drowned in the mud.
He tried to get out.
The more he tried to get out,
the more he felt himself sinking.
Soon he was in up to his waist.

7

Help at Hand

It was morning.
The mist had gone.
The sun was shining.

Dave was in the bog up to his chest.
His feet had found a firm bit.
He was all right for the time being.
But how could he get out?
What would happen if no one found him?

'Help!' he called.
'Help me!'

At long, long last, he saw a man
coming towards him.
Was it Nick? Had he come to look for him?

The man got nearer.
Dave saw it was the man from the shop,
with the beard and cap.

'Help!' said Dave.
'I'm stuck!'

The man looked at him.
'Got in a right mess, haven't you?' he said.
'I can't come any closer
or I'll sink in myself.
Stay there and I'll get help.'

He went away again.
He came back with two men and a rope.
They pulled Dave out.

They took him back to the village.
'You see, the moor can be a dangerous place,'
said the man with the cap.

'Yes,' said Dave. 'Well, thanks.'
He didn't say much more.
He felt a bit shy, now. A bit silly.

23

The man took him back to his house.
He gave Dave a cup of strong, sweet tea.
He lent him a pair of dry trousers
and a shirt.

'Thanks very much,' said Dave.
'I'd better go and get my friend now.
He'll be wondering where I am.'

8
The Photo

The sun was shining
as Dave walked back along the path.
Dave felt very happy.
He was glad to be alive.
He had nearly died but he was still here.

He would give up looking for the Beast.
It wasn't worth risking your life
just to make money.
He and Nick would go home.
Nick would be pleased.

He saw the tent ahead.
Nick wasn't outside it.
He must still be in there, thought Dave.
Too scared to come out
in case the Beast gets him!

Dave decided to play a trick on his friend.
He went up to the tent and gave a loud roar.
Just like the one they'd heard last night.
That would give Nick a shock!

There was no answer.

Dave pulled the tent flap open
and put his head in.

He was staring straight into
a big dark face with yellow eyes.
A big dark cat's face.
It was the Beast.

Behind it lay Nick –
or what was left of him.

27

The Beast opened its mouth.
It gave a roar.

Dave stepped back.
Without thinking, he raised his camera
and clicked.
It was the last thing he ever did.

Later, the men from the village
found the camera beside his body.

The picture of the Beast came out well.
It was in all the newspapers.